AROUND
HIGHWORTH
IN OLD PHOTOGRAPHS

Old Tithe Barn. Highworth.

Interior of Old Tithe Barn. Highworth.

Interior of Old Tithe Barn, Highwor

INTERIOR AND EXTERIOR VIEWS OF THE OLD TYTHE BARN, which stood on what is now the library car park facing Parsonage Farm. Parts of the foundations of the barn remained in situ until the development of the area in the late 1970s and early 1980s.

AROUND
HIGHWORTH
IN OLD PHOTOGRAPHS

COLLECTED BY
GRAHAM TANNER

ALAN SUTTON

Alan Sutton Publishing Limited
Phoenix Mill · Far Thrupp · Stroud · Gloucestershire

First published 1991

British Library Cataloguing in Publication Data

Around Highworth in old photographs.
I. Tanner, Graham, *1927–*
942.31
ISBN 0-7509-0005-9

Typeset in 9/10 Korinna.
Typesetting and origination by
Alan Sutton Publishing Limited.
Printed in Great Britain by
The Bath Press, Avon.

CONTENTS

AN ENGRAVING OF THE PARISH CHURCH of St Michael in the 1860s.

INTRODUCTION

The whole essence of Highworth and its environs was summed up by the late Poet Laureate John Betjeman in *First and Last Loves* (John Murray) where he wrote 'I have never seen Highworth given due praise in guide books for what it is – one of the most charming and unassuming country towns in the West of England. It is unspoiled by the vulgar fascias of chain stores, concrete lamp posts don't lean above its houses like seasick giants spewing orange light at night that turns us all to corpses, the roaring hideousness of main roads has left Highworth undisturbed. The only ugly things about it are some fussy red modern villas on the outskirts and too many electric light and telegraph wires zig-zagging across its High Street.

'Highworth is extraordinary because it has more beautiful buildings than it has ugly ones. It is mostly a Cotswold-coloured place of pale grey stone gathered round its church high on a hill, with a High Street and Market Place, a street at right angles, a Georgian doctor's house in red brick with a fine white wooden porch and doorway, and one more grand brick house – and these Georgian brick houses look as beautiful and ripe as autumn apples among all this silver stone of the streets. . . .

'When I am abroad and want to recall a typically English town, I think of Highworth. It is the sort of town read about in novels from Cranford to Miss MacNaughten. Ah, Highworth as a whole! Churches and chapels, doctors' houses, Vicarage, walled gardens with peas and plums, railway station, inns and distant cemetery, old shops and winding streets. We walked down one of these narrow lanes, between garden walls, that lead under archways into the High Street. (The only way to see a town is to go down every alley and see the backs of the houses.) Ivy-leaved toadflax with its little purple flowers hung over the stone, an uneven line of stone-tiled roofs and slate roofs, stone and brick chimney stacks, leaded windows under eaves, all these formed a base for the church tower. There was a sound of tea being cleared away in a cottage just near us. And suddenly with a burst the bells of Highworth church rang out for Evening Service. As though called by the bells, the late sun burst out and bathed the varied roofs with gold and scooped itself into the uneven panes of old windows. Sun and stone and old brick and garden flowers and church bells. That was a Sunday evening in Highworth. That was England.'

The earliest documentary record of the town appears in the Domesday Survey, the place-name suggesting an Anglo-Saxon origin. The entry indicates that 'From early days Radulphus, a priest, holds the church of Wide or Highworth, and three hides belong to it, which are not assessed. Two ploughlands: the priest occupies these with six borders and ten acres of meadow. It is worth 100 shillings.'

The town of Highworth was in effect founded in the middle years of the thirteenth century by the Earl of Devon who established some fifty burghers and a market around the church. The 'burgess' lands between the present High Street and Brewery Street are still a feature of the town, the other feature being the tythings of Eastrop and Westrop dating from the period immediately after 995 AD when the Danes overran north Wiltshire.

In the earliest days Highworth returned a member to Parliament. A writ was addressed to the bailiffs in the twenty-sixth year of Edward I's reign, to which no return was made. Elective franchise was never afterwards exercised, although writs continued to be sent to the bailiffs until the twenty-fourth year of Edward IV's reign. After that all rights of franchise were ceded to the Borough of Lechlade.

The Manor and ancient Hundred of Highworth are supposed to have been established by Charter of Edward I and even up to the beginning of the nineteenth century a court of pleas or court of barons was still being held for this Manor and Hundred, in which debts under the sum of forty shillings were recoverable.

There is no further documentary evidence until 1666, when the plague was at its height, the population of Highworth then being 3,821, whilst that of Swindon was only 2,500. Highworth at that time had a mayor and corporation, aldermen and council, and was a place of considerable importance. Aubrey recorded that at this time the Wednesday market was the largest in the county, but the influence of the plague and the Civil War led to the decline of the market, with business transferring to Swindon.

Highworth continued its quiet existence throughout the centuries, probably reaching its greatest eminence in the early nineteenth century. However, the decision of the Marquis of Ailesbury not to allow the Great Western Railway to pass through Savernake Forest and the Pewsey Vale led to the development of Swindon as a railway town, and the relative decline of Highworth. It remained a small country town with its country industries and fairs, the latter described by Alfred Williams, the 'Hammerman Poet' from South Marston (see p. 158): 'The fair was held in the market-place; but the whole of the principal streets were packed with booths and shows, swings, roundabouts, and other means of amusement; you could scarcely move for the crowds of people. Here were exhibitions of all kinds – of beast and birds, waxwork figures, model machinery, glass-making, cotton spinning, picture-galleries, and all sorts of things besides.

'All the men and boys who went to be hired wore whip-cord in their coats or hats; by this the farmer knew they were in search of a situation, and accosted them, and engaged them on the spot.'

I hope that the photographs in this book evoke the spirit of Highworth and its environs, so loved of writers such as Betjeman, Williams and Cobbett. Sadly, photographic evidence of all the town's activities is not readily available; in particular the Lammas Fair, the Flower Show, and Highworth in wartime. Additionally, two aspects of Highworth's fairly recent past which brought national interest, namely the 'Strike' school of 1937, and the exploits of the Highworth Wolves Cycle Speedway team in the late '40s and early '50s, are not represented here.

I would like to make a plea to readers of this book who have photographs of Highworth and district which are not reproduced here, to make these available to either the Highworth Historical Society or to myself, so that they might be reproduced for posterity in another edition of *Around Highworth in Old Photographs*.

Highworth

MARSH'S OUTFITTERS at the turn of the century, presently Allan & Harris, estate agents. 'Dapper' Marsh and his apprentices are on the right of the photograph. Oh, that Highworth could boast such an emporium now.

DAVIS THE UPHOLSTERERS in the High Street, now Jefferies DIY, dressed for the coronation of King George V in June 1911.

THE KING AND QUEEN dressed for the coronation of King George V in June 1911.

YEATES THE BUTCHERS (from 1918 to the 1980s trading as Reasons) similarly dressed for the coronation of George V in June 1911.

WILLIS'S GROCERS SHOP with its famed horse-drawn delivery van. Arthur Moulton is on the extreme right. Note the preponderance of advertising, in particular the enamelled 'street jewellery'.

WILLIS & SON GROCERS SHOP in the High Street (now Highworth DIY). 'Stacker' Willis is on the extreme right.

JOE REASON'S BUTCHERS SHOP (now Smith & Haines) dressed to show the Christmas stock in 1946. Despite rationing, at this time poultry was unrationed when available.

THE YOUNG MEN'S INSTITUTE in High Street (now Joanne's Boutique) dressed for the coronation of Edward VII. On the left is Arthur Willis, and on the right is Mr Head.

THE SITE OF THE POST OFFICE in the 1930s and '40s. During the early 1940s the post office effectively operated as the 'gateway' to the British Resistance. Postings to Coleshill House, the GHQ Auxiliary Units (the training centre for the British Resistance), were made to GHQ Auxiliary Units, c/o GPO Highworth, Wilts. The post mistress, Mrs M.A. Stranks, would telephone ahead to announce 'Some more of your lot are down here.'

HIGH STREET IN THE SNOWS of early 1947. Frank Turner of Turner's grocers stands at the entrance to his shop. Note the electricity poles (now thankfully removed) on the left of the street, and the gas lamps, sadly long removed.

A VICTORIAN PRINT OF THE HIGH STREET, showing the Cross Keys Inn at the extreme left. In existence before 1830, it closed in 1891, later to become the post office, then 'Clocky' Davis's shop, and now Cannon's betting shop.

HIGH STREET, LOOKING TO THE EAST from what has become Wise's corner. One of Teddy Drew's coaches can be seen at the far end of the street.

HIGH STREET FROM THE WEST, probably immediately post-war. Inigo House (on the right) was for many years the doctor's surgery. This early-eighteenth-century house is described by Nikolaus Pevsner as the finest house in Highworth.

HIGH STREET, AGAIN LOOKING WEST, this time photographed from approximately opposite the King and Queen. Note the small crowd of onlookers and Willis's delivery van outside the grocers shop.

HIGH STREET FROM ITS EXTREME WESTERN END in 1904. Note the ubiquitous schoolboy onlookers.

VIEW OF THE CENTRE FROM HIGH STREET, showing Jesmond House, then Higgs the tailors in the centre of the picture, with Colin Hicks's butchers shop to the left.

HIGH STREET FROM THE MARKET PLACE. Once again 'street jewellery' much in evidence on the front of Sturgess grocers shop, next to Lloyds Bank on the extreme left.

HIGH STREET FROM THE MARKET PLACE. Note the wrought iron balcony above what is now the Stroud & Swindon Building Society office.

HIGH STREET in the late 1940s. The lawn mowers on the left are outside Bartrop's, which sadly ceased trading in 1991.

HIGH STREET in the 1940s. Note the variety of implements displayed outside Bartrop's the ironmongers.

HIGH STREET FROM THE WEST. Davis the upholsterers is on the extreme left (now Jefferies DIY shop).

HIGH STREET TO THE EAST, probably taken from the roof of either Jesmond House, or the White House.

HIGH STREET FROM THE KING AND QUEEN in the 1940s. Electricity poles still disfigure the street.

SOUTH SIDE OF HIGH STREET in a relatively recent photograph.

NORTH SIDE OF HIGH STREET. Much in evidence is the enamelled 'street jewellery' on the front of Davis's.

MEET OF THE VALE OF WHITE HORSE HUNT in the Market Place, 1909.

MEET OF THE VALE OF WHITE HORSE (CRICKLADE) HUNT in the Market Place in the early 1950s.

PREPARATIONS FOR THE CELEBRATIONS to mark the coronation of King George V in June 1911, taking place in the Market Square.

THE OPENING OF THE HIGHWORTH WATERWORKS in 1904, replacing the reliance upon local wells and springs. Note the Highworth fire brigade in the centre of the photograph, and the preponderance of people wearing hats.

ANOTHER VIEW OF BOULTON & SON, GROCERS.

THE MARKET SQUARE in the early years of this century. Boulton's grocers shop is at the centre of the photograph. It was the scene of the town's livestock market for nearly seven hundred years; however in recent times the largely defunct market committee sold the square to the local council for a nominal fee. In more recent years there has been a revival, with a regular Saturday market.

A VIEW OF HIGH STREET FROM THE EAST in about 1910. The lamp standard in the centre of the Market Place is clearly visible just to the right of Marsh's shop.

THE MARKET PLACE IN THE 1930s. By now the gas lamp in the centre of the square has been removed. Silk's grocers shop (now the National Westminster Bank) is on the right-hand side of the square.

THE SARACEN'S HEAD HOTEL before the removal of the double doors to the coach entrance, and with its illuminated inn sign introduced by Arkell's brewery in the 1930s.

A RECENT VIEW OF THE SARACEN'S HEAD HOTEL and the podium. The somewhat alarming angle of the rowan tree in the centre of the podium was a predictor of its doom – it was uprooted during a winter storm.

CHURCH STREET OR SHEEP STREET, LOOKING WEST. The Rifleman public house occupies the present day site of the podium.

SHEEP STREET IN THE SNOW of the winter of 1946–7. By now the Rifleman Inn, on the left, is a private house.

SHEEP STREET FROM THE EAST END of the churchyard. The cobbled pavements are still visible in part of Vicarage Lane.

SHEEP STREET FROM THE CHURCHYARD, before the removal of unsightly electricity poles.

SHEEP STREET FROM THE EAST. By now the Red Lion public house had become offices, its licence having been transferred to the Goldfinger.

A VIEW FROM THE TOP OF THE CHURCH TOWER looking east over the valley of the River Cole, and on to Coleshill, Watchfield and the Berkshire Downs.

A VIEW OF THE SOUTH SIDE OF HIGH STREET, from the top of the church tower, showing Blandford Alley and Brewery Street.

A VIEW OF THE CENTRE TAKEN FROM THE CHURCH TOWER. On the left-hand corner of the centre stands Peapell's bakery; on the opposite corner we have Vernon Hicks's butchers shop, Jesmond House (Higgs the tailors), the White House, Highworth House, and the two farm cottages of Home Farm (at this time with a thatched roof). In the right-hand corner can be seen the rick yard of Home Farm, with open country extending to Hampton and Hannington.

AN AERIAL VIEW OF THE PARISH CHURCH of St Michael with the vicarage and Vicarage Lane behind the church. The since demolished Home Farm is almost directly behind the church tower.

AN AERIAL VIEW OF THE CENTRE OF THE TOWN taken from the south east in the 1960s, showing in the top left the development of the Home Farm housing estate.

SWINDON STREET, LOOKING NORTH. This view has not changed greatly even today, except for the loss of the two lime trees outside Ashman's butcher shop, and the dormer windows in what is now the Highworth fish shop.

SWINDON STREET, LOOKING NORTH from the School House. The cottages on the left were demolished in the 1970s to enable the roundabout to be built, and Brewery Street to be widened.

SWINDON STREET, LOOKING NORTH, soon after the Second World War.

SWINDON STREET, LOOKING NORTH. The television aerials indicate that this was the late '40s or very early '50s.

SWINDON STREET, LOOKING NORTH. Owen's garage is on the right, immediately before the two lime trees.

SWINDON STREET, LOOKING SOUTH. Warner's fish shop is the second house on the left, the façade having changed dramatically since the earlier photographs shown on p. 42 were taken.

SWINDON STREET, LOOKING SOUTH. The two lime trees outside Ashmans were a noted landmark, being for many years the site of the bus stop for journeys to Swindon.

Swindon Street. Highworth

SWINDON STREET, LOOKING SOUTH. Morse's bakery is on the extreme left, then the Co-op, and the Lime Tree Working Men's Club. This photograph is unusual, having been taken on a rainy day.

SWINDON STREET, LOOKING SOUTH. Note the fine example of a Wiltshire Waggon under the lime trees on the left. Baldwin's the coal merchants is on the extreme right.

SWINDON STREET, LOOKING SOUTH, before the pleasant double-fronted house on the left was converted into the original Co-operative stores.

JESMOND HOUSE, HIGHWORTH HOUSE AND HOME FARM COTTAGES. Note the thatched roof, unusual for Highworth, of the two cottages, which have since been reduced to one, and the absence of today's dormer windows.

WESTROP, LOOKING NORTH, taken from opposite the present Highworth sports shop, showing on the left Jesmond House, the White House, Highworth House, Home Farm cottages, the entrance to the farmyard, and Home Farm.

A VIEW OF WESTROP, LOOKING NORTH. The fine Georgian house on the extreme right was the Home Farm which was sadly demolished in the 1960s to make way for the Home Farm and Windrush housing estates.

A VIEW OF WESTROP TAKEN FROM THE CENTRE. To the left in the middle distance can be seen Home Farm, sadly demolished in the 1960s to make way for the Home Farm housing development. In the left foreground can be seen the two cottages immediately before the farm entrance, only one of which remains today.

THE JESMOND HOUSE HOTEL. By this time Vernon Hicks's butchers shop had been combined with the hotel.

A RELATIVELY RECENT SHOT of the Jesmond House Hotel. By now the original shop front of Vernon Hicks's butchers shop had been replaced by the new extension.

TURNPIKE COTTAGE and the turnpike gates at the top of Lechlade Hill. The gates were removed in the early 1870s. The chimney stack slightly to the right of the Plough Inn is that of the Highworth Gas Company.

TURNPIKE COTTAGE, on the corner of Lechlade Hill and Turnpike Road, was sadly demolished for road widening in 1975. The original building (see above) is on the left of the picture.

Turnpike Cottage, Highworth

ONE OF THE FEW THATCHED COTTAGES IN HIGHWORTH. The row of telegraph poles down Lechlade Hill do little to enhance the rural appeal of the photograph.

CHANTRY COTTAGE in the Lechlade Road. This could well be the oldest house in the town.

THE BOTTOM OF EASTROP HILL in the mid-1930s.

WESTHILL HOUSE AND HAMPTON HILL. The rural nature of the scene contrasts markedly with the situation today. Westhill House was at this time the residence of Sir Noel Arkell of Arkell's Brewery.

WEST HILL, LOOKING TOWARDS THE CENTRE. Except for the Co-op and gas lighting, very little has changed in eighty years.

WESTHILL HOUSE, built as the workhouse in the 1790s, was sold in 1847, when the Stratton St Margaret workhouse opened. It was then converted into the vicarage.

THE GARDENS OF WESTHILL HOUSE, then the home of Sir T. Noël Arkell.

THE VICARAGE, a gift in the early 1930s to the church from the Misses Hambridge of Queenlains Farm, Sevenhampton. In the late 1980s the building was sold by the Church Commissioners, and is now in use as commercial offices.

REDLANDS COURT, built as the home of James Arkell, the son of the founder of Arkell's Brewery.

EASTROP GRANGE. This was the home of H.W. Brown whose four sons, Gerald, Eric, Douglas and Kenneth, were killed in the First World War. They are commemorated by a stained glass window in the parish church. Until relatively recently the home of Graham Arkell of Arkell's Brewery, the Grange became the wartime home of an evacuated girls' boarding school.

WESTROP HOUSE, 1905. Built in 1818 by William Crowdy, Westrop House was visited by William Cobbett in 1827 when making his 'rural ride' from Highworth to Malmesbury along the old 'pack-horse' route.

A SEVENTEENTH-CENTURY DOVECOTE over a stable at Fresden Farm. The building is thought to date from 1650, which is the date inscribed on the door knocker.

A VIEW OF THE WAR MEMORIAL and the west entrance to the parish church in the late 1940s.

A VIEW OF THE PARISH CHURCH OF ST MICHAEL, probably taken from the roof of Highworth House.

THE SOUTH PORCH of the parish church of St Michael in about 1930.

THE PARISH CHURCH FROM THE WEST before the erection of the war memorial. The avenue of lime trees appears to have been rather severely pruned.

THE WAR MEMORIAL at the west gate of the parish church. Stone from the demolished tythe barn was used to provide the foundations for this memorial. The style of the wreaths laid on the memorial suggests the early 1920s.

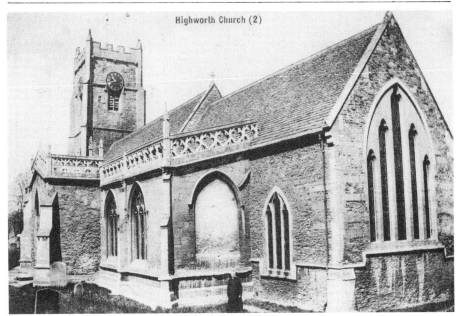

AN EXTERIOR VIEW OF THE PARISH CHURCH of St Michael, taken from the east end of the churchyard.

Highworth Parish Church

THE INTERIOR OF THE PARISH CHURCH, before the installation of the rood screen and new east window. The Warneford chapel is on the extreme right.

THE INTERIOR OF THE PARISH CHURCH from the chancel towards the west window. The Warneford chapel is behind the screen on the left.

A FLORAL BELL constructed for the first Festival of Highworth in 1972, and suspended at the west end of the church.

THIS TABLET WAS PLACED HERE BY MEMBERS OF THE WARNEFORD
FAMILY THROUGHOUT THE WORLD IN MEMORY OF
FLIGHT SUB-LIEUTENANT

REGINALD · ALEXANDER · JOHN WARNEFORD · V · C · R · N

CHEVALIER OF THE LEGION OF HONOUR AGED 23 YEARS · SON OF
THE LATE REGINALD WILLIAM HENRY WARNEFORD · Grandson of the
late Rev. T-L-J-Warneford Chaplain to the Forces in India · Gt Nephew of the late
Rev. Canon Warneford of Warneford Place · He was honoured by his King with
the Victoria Cross & by the French Nation with the Medal of the Legion of Honour for pursuing & destroying single-handed a Zeppelin Airship nr Ghent
in Belgium on 7th June 1915. He was killed 10 days later when flying in Paris
on 17th June 1915 & lies buried in Brompton Cemetery where the Nation has
shown its gratitude & recognition of his great achievement in the erection
of a Memorial by Public Subscription ✝

TO GOD ONLY WISE BE GLORY

A TABLET erected to the memory of Reginald Warneford VC in the Warneford chapel, St Michael's church (see pp. 122–3).

THE EAST WINDOW of the parish church, presented to the church by Miss Mary Hambridge of Queenlains Farm, Sevenhampton. The window depicts St Michael the patron saint killing the dragon, and includes the figures representing the caring vocations, together with the coats of arms of the bishoprics of which the parish had variously been a part, namely Bristol, Gloucester and Salisbury. During the Second World War the window was removed for safe keeping.

A CANNON BALL in the south transept of St Michael's church. This is reputed to be the one which struck the west tower during the attack on the church by Parliamentary forces under Fairfax on their way to Taunton after the Battle of Naseby (27 June 1645). Local legend suggests that the 'ball' was fired from a field in Hampton which is known locally as the 'humpty dumps' on account of its irregular surface.

HIGHWORTH STATION in the early years of this century. Note the 'street jewellery' of enamelled advertising signs on the end of the station building.

HIGHWORTH RAILWAY STATION early this century, again with enamel 'street jewellery' much in evidence.

THE HIGHWORTH 'BUNK' about to leave the station. Note the gas lighting, and horse droppings on the road to the goods bay, probably from Cook's coal cart.

THE 'BUNK' about to leave Highworth station. The station master's house is in the background, and cattle pens are immediately behind the second coach.

A PEACEFUL VIEW OF HIGHWORTH STATION from the area of the cattle pens, with the goods shed in the background. The evidence of a building in the top left-hand corner indicates the date as being in the mid-1950s.

HANGMAN'S ELMS, Shrivenham Road. Sadly the elms are no longer with us.

FRIAR'S MILL AVENUE. The avenue of elms was a casualty of Dutch elm disease in the late 1960s.

WOOLFORD'S YARD at the junction of Brewery Street and Shrivenham Road shown in a reproduction of Fred Richardson's water colour. The site, which is presently that of 'Threshold PSA' offices, shows a typical wheelwright's yard, which continued in operation until the early 1950s. In the background is the old National School, School House, and part of The Green.

THRESHING IN THE RICK YARD of Home Farm.

HAYMAKING AT WESTROP FARM, 1908. Top, l-r: A. Mouldon, ? Ealy. Bottom, l-r: P. Archer, J. Roberts, -?-, B. Seymour, -?- Gorton.

INSIDE THE LOOM SHOP at Highworth mat factory.

HIGHWORTH VORDA WORKS, Brewery Street.

A GREAT WESTERN RAILWAY LORRY collecting rolls of matting from the mat factory for transport to Highworth station and delivery by rail.

THE MAT FACTORY OFFICES, Brewery Street, in the 1950s. Woolford's yard is immediately to the right of this photograph.

THE SUN BREWERY, which gave its name to Brewery Street. Owned originally by the Rowden family in the early years of the nineteenth century, it later came under the ownership of William Hitchcock, then Thomas Hulbert, and finally Charles Wadley before being purchased by Ushers Brewery of Trowbridge, and closed down in 1918.

SIMON ILES, the Highworth dwarf, who lived in Vicarage Lane. Somewhat eccentric, he was given to waking people in the town by crowing like a cockerel in the early hours. He died in 1891 in the Highworth & Swindon Union Workhouse at Stratton St Margaret.

HIGHWORTH TOWN BAND in the late nineteenth century.

HIGHWORTH SILVER BAND 1953

22

HIGHWORTH SILVER BAND, 1953. Back row, l-r: W. Greengrass, C. Jefferies, G. Bassett, H. Haines, R. McLeod, G. Watts, A. People, A. Webb. Middle row: T. McLeod, M. Schulse, W. Gray, D. Haines, D. Watts, K. Woodward, R. Haines, J. Tame. Front row: R. Myers, J. Jefferies, A. Hill, S. Harman, D. Blackwell, D. Watts, F. Woodward.

HIGHWORTH SCOUTS at camp at West Bay, Dorset, 1937, on a visit to Weymouth. Back row, l-r: W.H. 'Pete' Gale (Headmaster, Highworth Council School), Muriel Tanner, Mrs E.C. Tanner, E.C. Tanner (Group Scoutmaster). Front row, l-r: F. Higgs, R. Fitchett, G. Tanner.

HIGHWORTH (ST MICHAEL'S) SCOUTS at camp, 1937. L-r: W. Gorton, -?-, F. Higgs, I. Trewhella, -?-, J. Slack, W.H. Gale (pointing), -?-, V. Trewhella, E.C. Tanner (Group Scoutmaster), Muriel Tanner.

HIGHWORTH (ST MICHAEL'S) SCOUTS, 1936. Back row, l-r: ? New, V. Trewhella (Assistant Scoutmaster), I. Trewhella (Assistant Scoutmaster), -?-. Middle row, l-r: -?-, -?-, R. Fitchett, -?-, E. Ryder, G. Tanner, W. Gorton. Front: -?-.

HIGHWORTH SCOUT TROOP, 1911.

HIGHWORTH FLOWER SHOW. A pillow fight is in progress. The date is unknown, but thought to be mid-1930s.

THE ROYAL ANTEDILUVIAN ORDER OF BUFFALOES' children's treat in 1922. Jack Archer on the right is wearing the top hat, and a Miss Gearing is dressed as a nurse on the extreme left.

HIGHWORTH TOWN FOOTBALL CLUB SUPPORTERS at Devizes for the final of the Wiltshire Senior Cup.

HIGHWORTH CRICKET CLUB DINNER, 1958. L-r: Maureen Tanner, Graham Tanner, Mrs Tony Skull, Tony Skull, Dennis Harding (Club Secretary and local policeman).

THE ZION CHAPEL'S SUNDAY SCHOOL TREAT at White Horse Hill in 1913. White Horse Hill remained a favourite venue for such trips until travel became easier in the mid-1930s. The Zion Chapel is now the United Reform Church.

THE ST JOHN'S GUILD OF BELLRINGERS, at the top of the church tower in 1910.

FREDDIE CROOME outside his grocers shop in the High Street. The premises are currently those of a hairdresser, Two's Company.

HOWARD AND SYBIL WHITE dressed for the pageant of the history of Highworth, presented by the junior school (now Southfields) in the mid-1950s. The photograph is of particular interest as the background shows clearly the Ministry of Aircraft Production bungalows built in 1941 to house the workers at the various aircraft factories in the district. Rivers Road and Newburgh Road, the site of these bungalows, is now occupied by Newburgh House, the shopping arcade, and Westrop Junior School.

HIGHWORTH BOARD SCHOOL (now Southfields Junior School). The field in the foreground, now the school's playing field, was then owned by John Reason.

HIGHWORTH JUNIOR SCHOOL (now Southfields Junior School) in the mid-1950s. The mat factory chimney shows clearly on the left of the photograph. This chimney was a considerable landmark in the town until it was demolished in the 1970s.

The Warneford School, Highworth. HRH.12.

THE WARNEFORD SECONDARY SCHOOL, opened in 1956. Its siting in the park commands an inspiring view of White Horse Hill and the Berkshire Downs. Its opening meant that the education of children of secondary age returned to the town for the first time since 1937, and evoked memories of Highworth's 'Strike' school of that period.

A HIGHWORTH JUNIOR SCHOOL CLASS in the mid-1940s.

ANOTHER CLASS AT HIGHWORTH JUNIOR SCHOOL at the same period.

A RECEPTION CLASS AT THE INFANTS SCHOOL, 1932. The school was built as the National School between 1835 and 1855 and closed in 1937 when the county council implemented the Hadon Report in the area, with the pupils moving across the road to the Board school, usually referred to as the 'big' school. During the Second World War the buildings became the First Aid Post and Light Rescue Centre of the Civil Defence, and are now used for commercial and residential purposes.

THE INFANT CLASS AT THE NATIONAL SCHOOL, 1901. Behind the gates to the playground can be seen the recently completed Board School.

CLASS 3 OF HIGHWORTH COUNCIL SCHOOL.

A CLASS FROM HIGHWORTH ELEMENTARY SCHOOL in 1923. On the extreme left is the headmaster Mr Ernest ('General') Booth, and on the extreme right is the class teacher Miss Moulton (later Mrs Mant). Note the class size: there are 41 in this photograph.

STANDARD III HIGHWORTH COUNCIL SCHOOL.

STANDARD III HIGHWORTH BOARD SCHOOL in the late 1890s.

ARMY MANOEUVRES, 1909. Horse-drawn pontoons of the Queen's Regiment are waiting in High Street.

MEN OF THE QUEEN'S REGIMENT resting in High Street. The café and Temperance Hotel, on the extreme right of the picture, remained as such until a few years before the Second World War.

THE TRANSPORT OF FOREIGN ATTACHÉS, with interested spectators in the Market Place. To the right of the Market House is Austin's Curiosity Shop, and 'Fishy' New's fish shop.

MEN OF THE QUEEN'S REGIMENT resting in High Street before moving on to 'defend' Coleshill.

A MAP OF THE ENCLOSURE AWARD for the parish of Highworth.

A CLOSE-UP OF THE ENCLOSURE AWARD MAP for the centre of Highworth. The enclosure of Highworth from the ancient open field system to the modern system of several ownership occurred during the period 1778–83.

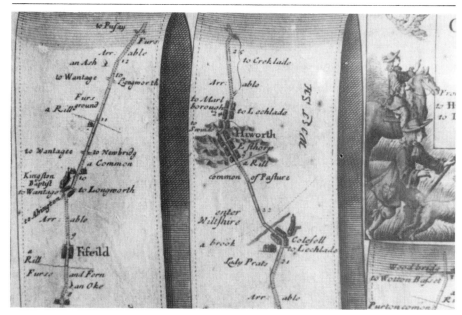

PART OF JAMES OGILBY'S MAP of 1675 showing the 'pack horse' route from Oxford to Bristol passing through Highworth.

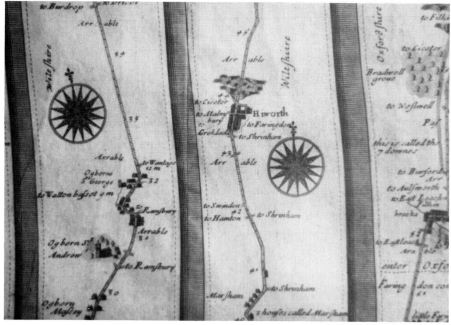

PART OF JAMES OGILBY'S MAP of 1675 showing the 'salt route' from Salisbury to Chipping Camden, and Highworth and its environs.

SOME EXAMPLES OF HIGHWORTH CIRCLES at North Lease Farm. Crop circles such as these become more readily visible during periods of drought, when the changes in the sub-soil tend to be reflected in the growth of the crops.

AN AERIAL PHOTOGRAPH SHOWING THE HIGHWORTH CIRCLES. Crop marks show evidence of enclosures dating from the twelfth and thirteenth centuries at Common Farm.

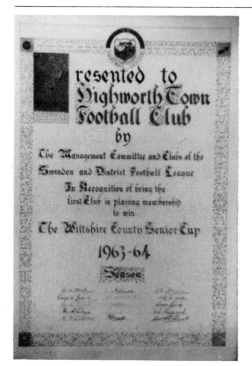

AN ILLUMINATED ADDRESS presented to Highworth Town Football Club by the Swindon & District Football League to recognize their achievement in winning the Wiltshire Senior Cup in the season 1963–4. Highworth Town was the first and only club in membership of the Swindon & District League to achieve this singular honour.

THE VICTORIOUS HIGHWORTH TOWN FOOTBALL CLUB after winning the Wiltshire Senior Cup. L-r: -?-, -?-, G. Robins, -?-, R. Haines, -?-, P. Webb, -?-, R. Jefferies, D. Haines, -?-.

HIGHWORTH TOWN FOOTBALL CLUB after defeating Devizes Town in the final of the Wiltshire Senior Cup at the County Ground, Swindon. Back row, l-r: R. Cuss, R. Jefferies, -?-, D. Cheesley (captain), R. Cooper, -?-, P. Scholes, -?-. Front row, l-r: J. Reid, -?-, -?-, M. Gardiner.

HIGHWORTH TOWN FOOTBALL CLUB, c. 1960. Back row, l-r: R. Gray, R. Haines, B. Smith. Middle row, l-r: -?-, A. Webb, C. Smith, P. Webb, P. Guy, J. Haggitt, H. Haines, D. Mapson. Front row, l-r: -?-, K. Webb, -?-, J. Smith, P. Brown, B. Higg, -?-.

HIGHWORTH TOWN FOOTBALL CLUB, 1960. Back row, l-r: D. Haines, J. Smith, D. McIver, P. Webb, P. Guy, R. Sumpter. Front row, l-r: C. Raisen, C. Smith, G. Robins, -?- Harris, P. Brown.

HIGHWORTH TOWN FOOTBALL CLUB, 1957. Back row, l-r: J. Haggit, A. Webb, J. Silk, F. Ockwell, H. Haines. Middle row, l-r: J. Farmer, R. Gray, P. Webb, R. Haines, L. Hutton, J. Jefferies. Front row, l-r: -?-, M. Tuckwell, J. Smith, P. Guy, N. Whittaker.

HIGHWORTH TOWN FOOTBALL CLUB, late 1950s. Back row, l-r: D. Haines, D. McIver, P. Webb, -?-, -?-. Middle row, l-r: -?-, G. Harris, ? Lewis, B. Higgs, R. Sumpter. In front: J. Smith.

HIGHWORTH TOWN FOOTBALL CLUB, 1909–10. Winners of the 'Advertiser Cup', and the Swindon & District Junior Cup. Back row, l-r: A. Willis, P. Evans, F. Hill, W. Jefferies, C. Richens, S. Rasey, E. Woodbridge, W. Silk. Middle row, l-r: C. Styles, G. Slack, A. Martin, H. Willoughby, W. Roberts. Front row, l-r: F. New, G. Smith, W. Avery, J. Brinklow, G. Haines.

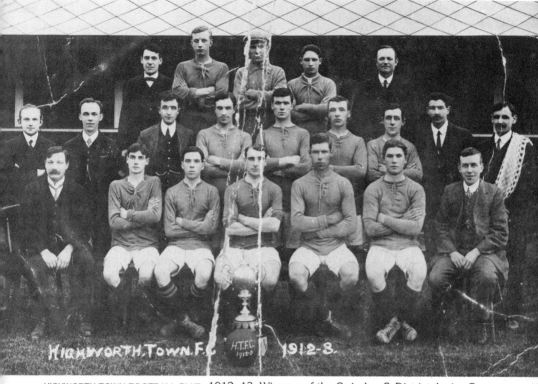

HIGHWORTH TOWN FOOTBALL CLUB, 1912–13. Winners of the Swindon & District Junior Cup. This photograph was taken in front of the old cricket pavilion in the recreation ground, which was destroyed by fire in the 1980s. Back row, l-r: P. Evans, A. Jefferies, W. Jefferies, F. Styles, J. Wheeler. Middle row, l-r: H. Clack, G. Woodward, F. Read, C. Styles, W. Acklin, J. Warwick, G. Smith, G. Allsopp, J. Midwinter. Front row, l-r: J. Winters, E. Clack, A. Smith, W. Avery, G. Slack, E. Smith, W. Willis.

WESTROP ROVERS FOOTBALL CLUB, 1927–8. Winners of the Cirencester & District League Division II, the Cirencester Hospital Cup and Langford six-a-side Cup. Back row, l-r: C. Hicks, J. Winter, F. Gorton, G. Watts, C. Lloyd, H. Cook, W. J. Winter, G. Mind, P. Jones. Middle row, l-r: W.R. Moulden, A. Cox, H. Hammans, S. Smith, G. Midwinter, G. Cook. Front row, l-r: E. Mapson, E. Smith, H. Attwood, J. Ackling, C. Cotton.

WESTROP ROVERS FOOTBALL CLUB, 1931–2. Winners of Division 1 Cirencester & District League.

WESTROP ROVERS FOOTBALL CLUB, 1960. Back row, l-r: -?-, John Jefferies, -?-, Alan Vockins, -?-, Denis Ackling. Front row, l-r: -?-, -?-, Frank Higgs, Jimmy Higgs, Len Johnson.

HIGHWORTH CRICKET CLUB, 1932. Winners of the Morse Shield. Back row, l-r: -?-, R. Bartrop, -?-, -?-, -?-, -?-, -?-, -?-. Middle row, l-r: J. Cook, W. Ackling, J. Owen, ? Wood, -?-, W. Woodbridge, H. Hammond. Front: -?-, -?-.

HIGHWORTH CRICKET CLUB, 1951. Back row, l-r: R. Brock, G. Furkins, W. Humphries, B. Cheadle, R. Archer, L. Cook, L. Cox, R. Bradford, Miss Cook, D. Smith, E. Boncey, Mr James. Front row, l-r: A. Skull, G. Tanner, J. Archer, J. Cook (captain), ? Macklin, ? Macklin, B. Archer.

'CAPTAINS COURAGEOUS'. Two long-serving captains of Highworth Cricket Club. On the left Joe Cook, on the right Jack Archer.

AWARD WINNERS AT THE HIGHWORTH CRICKET CLUB DINNER, 1958. Left to right: Graham Tanner, Doug Woodman, Ray Sumpter, Mike Bond.

The Outlying Villages Hannington, Sevenhampton, Coleshill, Inglesham, Stanton Fitzwarren

ST JOHN THE BAPTIST CHURCH, HANNINGTON. It was built by Slater & Carpenter in the period 1869–71, using many old parts, including the seventeenth-century walls, a fifteenth-century tower from which gargoyles gape, and an early thirteenth-century Norman doorway.

HANNINGTON HALL, built in 1653 by the brothers Raufe and William Freke, is a beautiful Elizabethan house with a pierced parapet, retaining the east front in its original state. Later additions, including a conservatory, were made in 1836, and the late nineteenth century.

THE EAST FRONT OF HANNINGTON HALL.

THE SCHOOL AT HANNINGTON, which was built for sixty children with Miss Charlotte Farnworth as mistress, closed in 1926 with the children transferring to Highworth. Up to the age of eleven transport was provided; over this age cycles were provided by the Local Education Authority.

THE JOLLY JAR, Hannington.

HANNINGTON in the 1930s. The outbuildings of Hannington Hall appear top left of the picture.

HANNINGTON in the 1930s.

HANNINGTON in the 1930s.

HANNINGTON in the winter of 1946–7. The building to the left was originally the Dog Inn until its closure by the magistrates in June 1907; it later became the post office. The building to the right is the village hall.

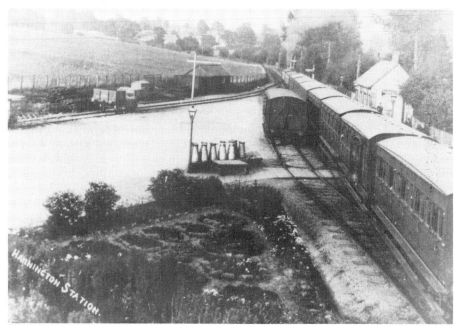

HANNINGTON STATION during the early years of this century when the line was at its busiest, as is evidenced by the length of the train, the neatness of the station garden, and the milk churns awaiting collection.

THE VALE OF WHITE HORSE (CRICKLADE) HUNT in full cry in a field below Hannington Hangings.

MANOR FARM, HANNINGTON WICK. A late seventeenth-century gabled manor house.

TADPOLE BRIDGE over the stripling River Thames at Hannington Wick.

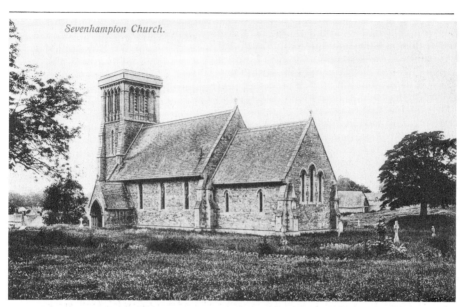

Sevenhampton Church.

THE CHURCH OF ST ANDREW, Sevenhampton, designed by W. Pedley and erected in 1864.

A MODERN AERIAL VIEW of the village of Sevenhampton, showing immediately below the church the remains of the earlier deserted village.

WARNEFORD PLACE, Sevenhampton. Originally the home of the Warneford family, it later became the home of Sir Frederick Banbury, and in the 1950s was purchased by Ian Fleming, who made extensive alterations to the building.

WESTMILL ON THE RIVER COLE at the boundary of Wiltshire and Oxfordshire (then Berkshire).

THE AVENUE TO WARNEFORD PLACE from the top of Sevenhampton Hill. Sadly the fine avenue of trees has succumbed to the ravages of time.

THE AVENUE OF ELMS, sadly destroyed in the late 1960s by Dutch elm disease, leading from the lodge at the bottom of Friar's Hill to Warneford Place.

A VIEW OF THE BERKSHIRE DOWNS from Friar's Mill Hill. The view is framed by the avenue of magnificent elms lost to the ravages of Dutch elm disease.

FLIGHT SUB-LIEUTENANT REGINALD WARNEFORD'S VICTORY over the Zeppelin LZ17 at Ghent, 7 June 1915 illustrated in this reproduction of a painting by G. Crosby. For this feat Warneford was awarded the Victoria Cross (see p. 60). The original painting hangs in the Imperial War Museum.

WARNEFORD'S GROUND CREW posing with his Morane Parasol at St Pol Aerodrome after the victory. The original print is signed G. Warneford.

REX WARNEFORD, a newly-qualified flight sub-lieutenant, posing at Hendon in front of a Maurice Farman II.

COLESHILL HILL FROM THE FOOT. The village, which was initially part of the estate of Lord Radnor, now forms part of the National Trust.

COLESHILL VILLAGE.

COLESHILL. The photographer once again attracts an audience.

VICTORIAN PRINTS of Coleshill House and its surrounding countryside.

THE PARISH CHURCH OF ST FAITH, COLESHILL.

Interior, Coleshill Church.

THE INTERIOR OF THE CHURCH OF ST FAITH, COLESHILL.

COLESHILL HOUSE FROM THE SOUTH WEST. Designed by Sir Roger Pratt, and built between 1650 and 1660, Coleshill House was one of the most splendid of seventeenth-century houses. Sadly destroyed by fire in September 1952, the house was the home of the Pleydell-Bouveries. Despite its architectural excellence, Coleshill House is probably better remembered for its role in the Second World War, when it became the centre for the training of the 'Auxiliary Units' which were to operate behind German lines in the event of Operation Sealion (the invasion of Britain) becoming a reality.

COLESHILL HOUSE.

COLESHILL MODEL FARM, which was built in 1852 for the Earl of Radnor. This ambitious project included barns, a granary, a rickyard, tramways, cutters, choppers, gravity-fed effluent disposal and livestock feeding.

COLESHILL UNITED FOOTBALL CLUB, 1956–7. Back row, l-r: L. Brown, J. Curley, -?-, A. Woodbridge, -?-, -?-, P. Whitman, F. Warren. Front row, l-r: ? Simpkins, ? Simpkins, G. Tanner, D. Caswell, -?-.

ST JOHN THE BAPTIST CHURCH, Inglesham.

ST JOHN THE BAPTIST CHURCH, Inglesham, in the grip of winter.

THE INTERIOR OF THE CHURCH OF ST JOHN THE BAPTIST, Inglesham. Standing a long way from the village, and reached by a lane leading to a farm, it is a tiny place filled with rare and unspoiled things. It was restored in 1888–9 by the Society for the Protection of Ancient Buildings, the driving force behind the restoration being William Morris of Kelmscot who 'loved it'.

INTERIOR OF ST JOHN THE BAPTIST CHURCH, Inglesham.

A VICTORIAN PRINT OF THE ROUND HOUSE at Inglesham. Built in 1790, the Round House marks the junction of the Thames & Severn Canal with the River Thames.

THE YOUTH HOSTEL, Lower Inglesham. It was opened in the mid-1930s, during the expansion of the Youth Hostel Association, to meet the needs of walkers. The hostel has recently been closed as the Association adjusts to the late twentieth century.

ANOTHER VIEW OF STANTON. The lane to the right of the photograph leads to the railway station.

A RURAL CORNER OF OLD STANTON.

THE CHURCH OF ST LEONARD, Stanton Fitzwarren, from the east.

THE GARDENS OF THE RECTORY, Stanton Fitzwarren, in the early years of the century.

THE SANCTUARY SCREEN, St Leonard's, Stanton Fitzwarren.

THE FONT AT ST LEONARD'S CHURCH, Stanton Fitzwarren. The carvings on the side of the bucket-shaped font represent the 'Triumph of the Virtues, with the aid of the Church, over a variety of curious hob-goblins termed Vices'.

STANTON HOUSE.

STANTON HOUSE was originally the home of the Trenchard family, and later that of Sir Geoffrey Tritton. It is now being developed as a conference centre.

STANTON STATION in the early 1940s, with Mr J. Meech the porter.

STANTON STATION, on the Swindon to Highworth Branch Line, was opened in 1883. This view was taken looking towards Highworth.

SECTION THREE

Blunsdon

THE COLD HARBOUR, BLUNSDON. The peaceful rural scene here contrasts strongly with the present-day traffic on the A419.

BLUNSDON'S MAIN STREET, with the school on the left-hand side.

THE HIGH STREET, BLUNSDON, with the Heart in Hand on the immediate left.

CHAPEL HILL, BLUNSDON.

CHAPEL HILL, BLUNSDON, and the Primitive Methodist church.

BLUNSDON HILL. Again, the contrast with today's dual carriage-way is extremely marked.

Stratton St Margaret

A TYPICAL LOCK on the Wiltshire and Berkshire Canal, which passed through parts of Stratton and South Marston.

THE OLD WILLOW TREE in Ermin Street. This particular tree was destroyed in a storm around the turn of the century.

ERMIN STREET in the early part of the century.

ARKELL'S BREWERY, Kingsdown.

KINGSDOWN CROSSROADS. The rural scene shown here contrasts vividly with the busy road junction of the present day.

THE OLD WHITE HART. Once again considerable imagination is required to relate this photograph to the present-day situation.

DORE'S ROAD, UPPER STRATTON. The thatched cottage on the left stands on the present site of the Wheatsheaf.

THE PLOUGH INN, Highworth Road, Stratton St Margaret, usually referred to as the 'Rat Trap', a name which of recent years has been officially adopted for the much modified and enlarged public house.

SPARKES CORNER, Stratton St Margaret. Sparkes' corner shop at the junction of Ermin Street and Swindon Road was a well-known local landmark.

UPPER STRATTON SECONDARY MODERN SCHOOL under 15 football team, 1954. They were winners of the Wiltshire Schools' Shield. Back row, l-r: L. King, D. Gray, D. McIver, R. Haines, -?-, -?-, -?-. Front row, l-r: R. Woodruff, G. Timms, C. Packer, ? Lane, M. Morris.

UPPER STRATTON SECONDARY MODERN SCHOOL under 13 football team, 1952. Back row, l-r: M. Morris, -?-, R. Haines, ? Large, -?- Carter. Front row, l-r: ? Lane, D. Gray, B. Gee, G. Timms, -?-, ? Bird.

STRATTON REFORM FOOTBALL CLUB, 1921–2. Winners of the Swindon Advertiser Cup, Swindon & District League, Dr Elliott Cup. Back row, l-r: -?-, -?-, A.Mapson, -?-, -?-. Second row, l-r: F. Willoughby, A. Davies, J. Packer, A. Church, E. Herring, F. Savery, A. Grant, S. Hankivell. Third row, l-r: A. Bown, H. Bown, E. Hatherall, S. Moulding, S. Bown, G. Edmonds, A. Staples. Front: H. Shute, R. Hinchcliffe.

AN ATHLETICS CLASS in action at the Kingsdown High School, c. 1965.

DON RICKETS of the Upper Stratton Secondary Modern School winning the Junior Boys 100 yards at the English Schools' Athletic Association's Championships at Port Sunlight, Cheshire, 1949. He won in a new record time of 10.4 seconds, removing 0.4 seconds from the previous record. For this performance Don was awarded the medal for the most outstanding performance.

BRENDA GILL of Green Road, Upper Stratton, who in 1963 became the first member of the Swindon Athletic Club to represent Great Britain & Northern Ireland in an international match. Brenda was a member of the winning British team in a pentathlon international versus Holland & Belgium.

South Marston
and the Airfield

THE INTERIOR OF THE CHURCH of St Mary Magdalen, South Marston.

AN AERIAL VIEW of the Phillip & Powis shadow factory under construction at South Marston in early 1940. After manufacturing the Miles Master III Advanced Trainer, the factory produced the Vickers Supermarine Spitfire during the latter stages of the war.

THE MILES MASTER III ADVANCED TRAINER, produced in the early 1940s at the South Marston factory of Philip & Powis Aircraft Limited.

SHORT 'STIRLING' FOUR-ENGINED BOMBERS under construction at South Marston.

PART OF THE WORKFORCE at Flight Sheds 2, South Marston, who were engaged in the building of the Short 'Stirling', the first of Britain's four-engined bombers during the period 1941–4. The parent factory of Short's at Rochester, Kent was severely damaged by Luftwaffe raids in 1940, and production of the Stirling was switched to the Swindon and Belfast areas.

DELIVERY OF THE LAST SUPERMARINE SPITFIRE from the South Marston factory.

SUPERMARINE ATTACKERS under construction at South Marston.

SUPERMARINE ATTACKERS on South Marston airfield. The control tower can be seen in the right background, and a De Haviland Dragon Rapide communications plane in the centre background.

A SUPERMARINE SWIFT carrying out an 'engine run' in the 'silencing pen' at South Marston in 1954. The advent of supersonic aircraft, and the resultant breaking of the sound barrier, caused considerable problems both locally and nationally. The installation of such 'silencing pens' was an attempt to reduce this problem.

THE VILLAGE SCHOOL at South Marston.

LONGLEASE FARM, South Marston.

AN ALAN-WILLIAMS STEEL TURRET of the type provided for the defence of the Phillip & Powis airfield at South Marston.

A PILLBOX of 1940 vintage alongside the River Thames. These formed part of the so-called GHQ (General Head Quarters) line which ran from Bristol to Maidstone, following the River Thames, with pill boxes from Radcot to St John's lock at Lechlade.

ALFRED WILLIAMS, the 'Hammerman Poet' of South Marston. He is famous for his studies of local life, such as *Villages of the White Horse, Life in a Railway Factory* and *A Wiltshire Village*, with its evocative description of Highworth and the Lammas Fair.

AVRO ANSON from RAF Station, Watchfield.

ENTRANCE TO RAF STATION, Watchfield whose role was described by Michael Bowyer in *Action Stations 6*: 'Watchfield's contribution to the winning of the war is impossible to assess, but it played an important part in improving the safe return of many an operational crew.' Watchfield was No. 1 Blind Approach School.

THE CONTROL TOWER and hanger at RAF Watchfield.

ACKNOWLEDGEMENTS

I would like to thank the undermentioned for their help and assistance in the preparation of this book: my wife Maureen for her patience and forebearance not only while preparing this book, but in many visits to postcard fairs etc.; Mr Brian Earl for his continued help and assistance in the reproduction of photographs; Mrs Andrée Amos for her secretarial skills; members of the Highworth Historical Society (in particular Dr Brian Lawton and Mr John Bailey); Mr Rodney Haines; and Highworthians too many to mention, whose enthusiasm for Highworth continues to support me.

My thanks are also due to Mr Derek White, Mr Fred Stevens and Mrs Moxon for continuing to find postcards of Highworth and district for me to add to my collection.